Navigating Pastoral Transitions

Navigating Pastoral Transitions

A Parish Leader's Guide

Marti R. Jewell

LITURGICAL PRESS
Collegeville, Minnesota

www.litpress.org

Cover design by Stefan Killen Design. Cover photo © Thinkstock.

1	2	3	4	5	6	7	8	9

Library of Congress Cataloging-in-Publication Data

Jewell, Marti R.
  Navigating pastoral transitions : a parish leader's guide / Marti R. Jewell.
    pages cm
  Includes bibliographical references.
  ISBN 978-0-8146-3806-4 — ISBN 978-0-8146-3831-6 (ebook)
    1. Catholic Church—Clergy—Relocation—Study and teaching.
  2. Change—Religious aspects—Catholic Church—Study and teaching.
  I. Title.

BX1912.J49   2013
254'.02—dc23   2013019769

Contents

Preface

The Archdiocese of Chicago and Loyola University Chicago funded this guide through a grant from the Lilly Endowment, Inc. *Sustaining Pastoral Excellence* (SPE) program. Dedicated to finding and sustaining excellent pastoral work in several U.S. Christian denominations, SPE helped the Archdiocese and University found INSPIRE. The INSPIRE project promotes pastoral excellence in parishes of the Archdiocese. Its acronym summarizes its mission: to Identify, Nurture, and Sustain Pastoral Imagination through Resources for Excellence. Serving parish staffs throughout the Archdiocese, INSPIRE helps them develop collaborative expressions of excellence in pastoral leadership.

On behalf of the Archdiocese of Chicago Department of Personnel Services, the Office for Lay Ecclesial Ministry submitted a proposal to INSPIRE recommending a Pastor Transition Study Team to explore the challenges and opportunities inherent in pastor transitions. The task force formed the following question to express their singular mandate: Can we find better ways for priests to make their way to new parishes as pastors?

Subsequently the quest was extended to see how parish staff and parishioner leaders can best work through this difficult time in the life of the parish, and booklets were developed for these groups.

Members of the Study Team designed and implemented surveys of pastors, parish staffs, and parishioner leaders in the Archdiocese of Chicago who had recently experienced a pastor change. The team is grateful for the participation of ordained and lay leaders who generously contributed their observations and insights.

The following persons contributed time and effort to the Archdiocese of Chicago Pastor Transitions Study Team:

Mark Bersano, Assistant Director, INSPIRE
Ralph Bonaccorsi, Office of Conciliation
Rev. James Donovan, Secretary, Priest Placement Board
Rev. Vincent Costello, Co-Vicar for Priests
Daniel Gast, Director, INSPIRE
Rita Kattner, DMin, Office for Councils,
    Christ Renews His Parish
Kathleen Leggdas, Director, Office of Ministerial Evaluation
Carol Walters, Director, Lay Ecclesial Ministry
Cathy Walz, Office for Catechesis and Youth Ministry

Commissioned Author:
Marti R. Jewell, DMin
Assistant Professor of Theology,
    University of Dallas/School of Ministry
Director Emeritus of the Emerging Models
    of Pastoral Leadership Project

The author acknowledges and thanks for their support and insights:

Sal Della Bella, Director of Evangelization,
    Archdiocese of Louisville
Theresa Khirallah, SSND, Director of Ministries,
    Diocese of Dallas
Mark Mogilka, Director of Stewardship
    and Pastoral Services, Diocese of Green Bay
Lauri-Anne Reinhart, Director of Religious Education,
    Reno, Nevada
Brian Reynolds, Chancellor/Chief Administrative Officer,
    Archdiocese of Louisville

Introduction

The news has arrived. Maybe you knew it was coming, maybe you didn't, but here it is. Your parish is going to have a new pastor. Questions tumble through your mind. Who is coming? Will the parish have any say in the matter? Will you like the new pastor? Are things going to change? What are parish leaders supposed to do? If you recognize yourself in this scenario, then this guide is for you.

> "I believe that this is one of the important and positive results of the Council: the co-responsibility of the entire parish, for the parish priest is no longer the only one to animate everything."
> *Pope Benedict XVI*[1]

Every year parishes across the country experience pastor transition. In many dioceses pastors are moved after terms of six or twelve years. Some pastors retire. Others are reassigned for a variety of reasons. No matter why a transition happens, transfers affect the life of the parish. While each parishioner experiences these changes personally, the whole community goes through a process with some very predictable elements that are shared in this guide.

As a parish leader, whether serving on a council, board, commission, committee of the parish, or in some other designated role, you are in a unique position to support parishioners and staff as they say good-bye to one pastor and hello to another. Armed with some key information, a few strategies, and a vision for how this time can go well, you will be able to support your community during this time of transition.

1

There are things you can do to positively impact this transition time. Whether you are excited about the pastor coming, grieving the loss of your current pastor, or uncertain about the new pastor bringing his own ideas and ways of doing things, know that your leadership matters. However you respond you can count on this being a time when the parish culture opens to new possibilities. A new spirit and new opportunities will emerge. How you will be a part of them is up to you!

The Goal of *A Parish Leader's Guide*

This guide invites you to take an active part in the pastoral transition process. As a parish leader, you will be asked to support the transition even as you personally deal with changes as they happen—whether you like the changes or not.

Rather than letting events dictate your experience, you will be encouraged to recognize what is happening to you and to the community and take positive steps to move through the stages of change. What will matter the most, as you move through this time of transition, is its impact on your faith community. People matter. Individuals matter. You matter!

In this guide you will find an explanation of the transition process and what to expect from the time that you and your parish receive the announcement of the pastor change to beginning your work with the new pastor. Throughout *A Parish Leader's Guide* you will be offered a variety of strategies for walking with your parish through the transition along with personal reflection questions, group discussion questions, resources, and checklists of tasks that lie ahead. Many of these tested and time-honored strategies come from parish leaders who recently experienced a pastor transition themselves.

You can use this guide for best practices and self care. You will be invited to look at the spirituality of this change, at the empty tomb, on the road to Emmaus, in the upper room, and moving out in a new Pentecost just as the first disciples did. Following that you will see the components of change and how they are found in the experience of pastor transitions. You may want to read the guide with other parishioners and lay leaders so that you all develop a common understanding of what happens during a pastor transition.

Companion texts—one for your pastor and another for parish staff—offer the potential for lively conversations among everyone involved in the transition as they follow in the footsteps of the early Church, when amazing, confusing, and finally inspiring and life-giving transitions first played out. As you move forward in a pastor transition, you will be able to root this critical time in prayer and so nourish the mission of the parish.

As supplemental resources, the three books of the *Navigating Pastoral Transitions* series are not intended to replace the polices and procedures of your own diocese or archdiocese. Links to many such documents are provided at www.litpress.org/pastoraltransitions /resources.

It's Happening on My Watch!

As a parish leader during a significant transition, you may find yourself in an unenviable position. People may turn to the pastoral council, the finance council, or any one of the parish committees, expecting them to step up and do whatever needs to be done. You may hear people say there is nothing parishioners and parish leaders can do, since everything has come down

> The Lord appointed seventy [-two] others whom he sent out ahead of him in pairs to every town and place he intended to visit.
>
> *(Luke 10:1)*

from "on high"—meaning, of course, from the diocese. But people are not content with that; they have questions and rumors to share, and they want answers. What can parish leaders do during a pastor transition?

This guide relies largely on the work of William Bridges who writes extensively about organizational and personal change.[2] Bridges reverses the assumed "beginning, middle, end" process to one calling us to recognize that what we have known must end before we can fully embrace the new. He offers these three, often overlapping, stages:

Ending: A time for letting go and making space for what is coming, for saying good-bye to persons but also to the way things used to be.

Neutral Zone: A middle ground time when things are in flux, sometimes discomfiting and anxiety provoking but more than a waiting time. Leaders can make this a period of productive activity, exploration, testing, and preparation. The middle ground is a neutral zone that can invite exploration, innovation, discovery, and learning.

New Beginning: A time of recognizing that you have crossed an important portal. New persons arrive, new roles begin, and new practices get put in place.

You should note one more thing at this point: The process Dr. Bridges suggests doesn't necessarily play out in orderly sequence. Experientially, even though one of the stages is foremost in your awareness, you seem to always have all three stages going on simultaneously. Additionally, be aware that people in the community won't proceed through the transition in lock-step conformity. As a parish leader, for instance, you may perceive yourself arriving in the "new beginnings" stage while some parishioners may have just begun grieving, or resisting, or letting go.

A Spirituality of Parish Leadership in Times of Change

The birth of our Church was just such a time. There was an ending. Jesus had been killed, had died on the cross, and now there were reports of an empty tomb. When Mary and the women did not find Jesus' body in the tomb, they went to tell the disciples. Peter ran to the tomb to see for himself. The reports were true! It was beyond belief. How could this have happened? People felt scared and confused.

> They found the stone rolled away from the tomb; but when they entered, they did not find the body of the Lord Jesus. *(Luke 24:2-3)*

At about the same time there were two disciples on the road to Emmaus. They had been in Jerusalem during the crucifixion and now were returning home. They were talking about all that happened. Maybe they were wondering how everything they had been involved in had disappeared so quickly. What were they going to do? How could they explain it all?

Are these disciples not like you when faced with a pastor transition? You know things have changed, but you can't see yet how it will affect you and your community. But the two disciples discovered they were not alone. Nor are you.

> Then beginning with Moses and all the prophets, he interpreted to them what referred to him in all the scriptures. *(Luke 24:27)*

Jesus walked with them, although at first they thought him a stranger, explained things to them, just as he would explain to the worried disciples in the upper room. He heard their doubts and invited them to think things through. Ever patient, Jesus reassured the disciples, assuaging their fears and doubts. Back to Jerusalem the two went, sharing the good news. During the in-between time Jesus had not abandoned them.

> Then he said to them, "Why are you troubled? And why do questions arise in your hearts?" *(Luke 24:38)*

The life the disciples had known with Jesus was over, and they hid themselves. Little did they understand what an incredible new life was about to begin! They would learn to believe and gather courage.

As your pastor leaves and a new one arrives, you are assisting a new stage in the life of your parish. You may be uncertain about what it is coming, but you can be assured that Jesus will walk with you and that you can find him in those with whom you gather at the Lord's table.

Transition Pathways: From Endings to Beginnings

The process of changing pastors involves endings, middles, and beginnings. You find yourself being asked to let go of what has been, saying good-bye to the pastor you have known. Then follows a period of uncertainty as you prepare to meet your new pastor and begin getting to know him. Finally, you will notice, with the arrival of the new pastor, your parish really has begun moving into a new phase in its life. What this will look like in your parish remains to be seen. What you can count on is that change and excitement will be in the air!

When the diocese announced that your parish would change pastors, you may have been surprised because the transition was unexpected. Possibly your parish knew this change was coming and had already begun to prepare. There is a flurry of activity as plans for your pastor's departure are made. Lots of conversations begin as people anticipate the new pastor's arrival. It is almost as if you can hear one door closing and another opening.

As a parish leader, you and your colleagues may be informed first and will begin the transition pathway before the rest of the parish. The stages of transition addressed in this guide could be read as if one follows the other in a neat and orderly fashion. As you well know, life is rarely that neat and orderly! You will find that these stages overlap one another, and even if you began the transition process before the rest of the parish and are already working through the stages, you will need to be patient when those around you begin the process.

As parishioners learn of the transition, you will notice a variety of reactions. Passions may run high. Anxieties may surface. Some people may seem very excited; some mourn; others talk about possibilities. You may not understand why people act as they do, but all of these things are part of the process of change in communities. The truth is, in a parish system, everyone is affected one way or another. As a parish leader, what will you be noticing?

Some parishioners will greet the transition, perhaps with a little nervous energy about the change but generally pleased with what is happening. They find themselves curious, excited, and hopeful about the possibilities before the parish.

Many people will appear and act neutral toward the change. They anticipate welcoming the new pastor and going on as before. While they will see a new presider at liturgy, they do not feel overly stressed by the change.

Still others will be unhappy with the change. Some may even plan to follow the departing pastor to his new parish. Others will be sad that their pastor is leaving. They could be upset about the newly assigned pastor and unable to accept what has happened. They might stay, causing some uproar with their dissension for a time. Some may leave to seek another faith community. Nevertheless, everyone in this mixed community will need care in the months ahead.

> Parishes are communities of faith, of action, and of hope. They are where the gospel is proclaimed and celebrated, where believers are formed and sent to renew the earth.
> *Communities of Salt and Light, United States Conference of Catholic Bishops*

Moreover, you get to decide which group you will be a part of and how you want to interact with the parish during this time. Each of these responses is normal and to be expected. How you react to them is what matters. Whatever you decide, the important thing for you to remember is that we are all God's people and everyone deserves to be treated with respect.

Notes

1. Pope Benedict XVI, "Meeting With Clergy," *Origins* 37, no. 11 (August 16, 2007): 190.

2. William Bridges, *Managing Transitions: Making the Most of Change*, 3rd ed. (Cambridge, MA: Da Capo Lifelong Books, 2009).

Begin with Endings

Ironic isn't it? But this is how change starts. What *was* is ending, and you need to begin letting go of what used to be. A critical task in the beginning is to minister to endings, to support everyone as they say good-bye. Often facilitated by parish leaders, everyone will engage the pastor's leave-taking one way or another. A well-planned and elegantly offered good-bye serves both the transitioning pastor and, perhaps even more so, the community. All are served by a farewell in which each person can participate.

First Reactions

At first you may experience resistance to the announcement, a "This can't be happening to us!" feeling. Resistance is the mind's way of allowing you to catch up with change and it shows up in a lot of ways.

Some people find themselves surprised by an emotional response to the news. Some may become angry, arguing with every detail of the transition or wanting to write an angry letter to the bishop. For most, though, resistance will be a little less intense, but they may nevertheless express anxiety or concern. Some may worry that the person who knows what is happening in their lives will no longer be available. Will the new pastor be able to understand what they have been going through? Other concerns may be much more pragmatic, such as wondering who will preside at a daughter's wedding or baptize a baby. Some will hesitate to move on with commitments: will the parish be able to continue planning the Fall Festival?

During transitions some people move into high gear. It's one way they can soothe the anxieties they feel. They have a "let's get going" attitude, and they express excitement for new possibilities that present themselves. Maybe they will be happier with the way a new pastor presides at liturgy or understands social action.

Others move to the opposite end of the spectrum, surprising everyone and perhaps even themselves by trying to slow things down. Suddenly that unfinished committee project seems less important to complete! Some people may simply disappear for a while. These are all normal reactions as the transition proceeds. Be patient with each other. This is all a part of the process.

As a parish leader you can expect to see and feel a variety of emotional responses, and they may all come to you at the same time! Whatever you are feeling, with change comes some confusion because you don't know exactly what you are supposed to do. This may not be a comfortable place to be in. You may find yourself trying a number of things in response to the announcement, questioning yourself and others, wondering what you can do to make this work for yourself and the parish. Do you need to be more involved, or less? What is your responsibility as a parish leader? Where do we go from here?

Getting Started

Once the announcement has been made about a new pastor, there are a number of things that need to be done fairly quickly. Consult with your departing pastor and the staff. Be sensitive to their feelings and needs. Offer to help them develop ways to move the parish through this farewell period. For everyone this will involve reestablishing and sustaining personal balance. To serve the community's sense of balance, honesty and openness can do a lot to calm anxiety.

Provide frequent communication using simple, straight-forward messages. As early as possible, coordinate with the parish staff to communicate the reasons for the transition. Clear communication can help reduce confusion and anxiety. How those reasons are shared will make a very big difference in how the new pastor will be received. Remember, in the face of little or no communication, imaginations take over and rumors and gossip can become rampant. Leaders learn not to underestimate the parish grapevine!

Use all modes available to keep the community updated about the transition.

- Make announcements in the bulletin, at Mass, to committees, commissions, boards, and councils.

- Send group texts or e-mails that can have a personal touch, especially in a smaller parish.

- Update or create parish web site, Twitter, and Facebook pages.

- Conduct, when possible, in-person conversations that can be perceived as powerful, welcome gestures.

Begin planning the pastor's good-bye. Be sure to find out how the pastor and staff want to proceed. You will find strategies and suggestions listed below. Doing this step well will make a real difference in how the parish moves forward.

Find ways to honor the past and be clear about what will continue. Compose a positively worded prayer that all groups may use at the start of their meetings. Celebrate the good things and acknowledge the challenges ahead, so that you can be ready to figure out the next steps for growing the parish.

> Remember not the events of
>   the past,
>   the things of long ago
>   consider not;
> See, I am doing something
>   new!
>   Now it springs forth, do you
>   not perceive it?
>   *(Isa 43:18-19a)*

What You Can Do

As you say good-bye to your pastor and begin to anticipate what is coming, a big part of your task is simply to live in and hold the space. Begin listening to what is going on inside of you, to others, and to the community as a whole.

- Don't say good-bye too fast. Savor what was, determine to work with your pastor until he actually leaves, and **allow the process to move at its own pace**.

- Find a way to **claim what was the best part of the past** so that you have permission to move forward with a sense of what is important to you.

- Don't spend time criticizing or remembering only the problems. It is not necessary to negate the past in order to give yourself permission to **accept the future**.

- Don't hold on. When people leave, we must be willing to **let them go**.

- As you are able, **finish projects and follow through** with responsibilities.

- Examine whether you need to **resolve any healing or forgiveness issues** before your pastor leaves. Don't leave yourself with any regrets.

- **Ritualize the leave-taking** by writing a personal note, or finding some way for a personal good-bye that is true to the level of relationship you have had with your departing pastor. This can mean a great deal to you both.

Questions for Personal Reflection

1. How do I understand the change I am experiencing?

2. What is really important to me that I really hope my parish can hold on to?

3. How am I reacting privately and publicly to the impending change?

4. Am I comfortable sharing my experience of this ending with others?

5. Am I denying emotions, avoiding people, doing too much?

6. How am I caring for those around me?

7. Am I setting good boundaries and being responsible in my own conversations?

Questions for Group Discussion

1. Does the community understand the change and why it is happening?

2. How is our parish moving into the process of transition? What does this look like?

3. How are we working with the pastor and staff to prepare for this transition?

4. Have we put a transition team in place?

5. Is information being accurately and frequently communicated to the community?

6. What are the secondary changes?

7. What are some consequences that no one thought about?

8. How can we say good-bye to our pastor? Have we asked him what he wants?

9. How would we like to ritualize his leave-taking?

Wandering Through the Middle Ground

Being in the middle ground is a little like jumping across the Grand Canyon on a motorcycle in slow motion. We can all imagine that moment in midair, canyon rims left behind or far in front. You feel as if there is no safety net below you. And while the time to make the jump is really very short, in that moment, when you are far above the canyon floor, you may feel as if you have moved into a time of suspended animation. There seems to be much that is up in the air!

It is important, however, to find middle ground, plant your feet firmly on its pathway, and help others do likewise. All must realize they are not alone. Both sooner and later, the entire community experiences this critical "not yet" time. Not only is it a critical time, it is a period rich with potential and opportunity. No matter how much everyone may want it to be over, it is important not to rush. Go easy. Be realistic about what needs to happen and how soon. Perhaps the kindest thing you can do for yourself is give the process time.

Be willing to listen and encourage others to listen to each other. Be empathetic to the community during this passage. Many parishioners will have opinions, concerns, some confusion, or ideas to share. As a parish leader you will want to encourage support of one another as the community moves through the middle ground. During this in-between experience, a primary leadership act is ensuring that parish life continues as fully and routinely as possible, while all the time looking ahead with hope and positive anticipation.

Some parishes learn only that their pastor will be up for transfer and that a new pastor will be named later. When that announcement does happen publicly, lay leaders can help pave the way for their departing pastor's graceful exit and the new pastor's equally graceful arrival. In the best of circumstances, this is a collaborative work of departing pastor, parish staff, and lay leaders.

It is important at first to give a name and a face to the new pastor. Some parishes have found it helpful to create introductory opportunities: a simple note in the bulletin, a mention by the current pastor that he and the incoming pastor will meet from time to time as the days move forward. Could there be a video blog on the parish web site? What could be a positive way to allow people to learn about the new man who will become their pastor?

Four Steps for Traversing Middle Ground

In any sizable community, different persons approach challenges in different ways. Some need to know *why* things are happening as they are. These are the people who will best address the question of purpose. Some are energized by understanding *what* is happening; they can help others picture what is going on. Others need to know *how* this is going to happen and can assist in the planning and caring for the parish during the transition. Still others need to know *who* is involved in the process and find their roles in the transition.[1] There are many opportunities to meet these needs and to engage parishioners in this middle ground.

Based on the work of Dr. William Bridges, here are four steps that staff and parish leaders can use to help the community move through the middle ground and launch new beginnings: securing purpose, holding up a picture, developing a plan, and providing parts to play.[2]

1. Securing Purpose

People need to know that there is a context, a larger vision at work in this change. Communicating rationale assists those people who need to know *why*. Knowledge about why this is happening also serves to stabilize the community. Most often the transition happens because the pastor has completed his assigned term in the parish. Over the years, bishops and priests themselves have learned to value limited terms of service. They understand that letting go might be painful, but at the same time productive of growth and life-giving to priestly ministry as well as to parishes.

There are other circumstances. The pastor may be ready to retire. He may have been called to a new role where his particular gifts are greatly needed. Certainly there are times when unforeseen situations create abrupt reassignments or when the reasons for the changes are complicated. Regardless, as much as possible, clearly and succinctly communicate reasons for these events. How change is communicated affects the message people hear as much as its actual content. Muster all the charity, transparency, and clarity possible. Studies have shown that, for a parish to move forward, changes affecting the entire community must be addressed.[3] Trust people to be able to handle the information they need.

Remember the purpose of the parish. It is possible that, in the course of events, a parish community loses sight of the calling of a parish. Recalling the true mission of the parish at this time can help people move forward. What is the purpose of a parish? Do you have a mission statement? Does the parish have a story or self-image that is important?

Parishes are much more than the pastor. They are communities of disciples who come together to care for one another, be strengthened in their faith journey, celebrate together in worship, pass on their faith, and take it out into the world. The health of a parish is not dependent on any one pastor or any one group of parish leaders to do these things. But it is dependent on how well they are able to be a welcoming Eucharistic community.[4]

A community can effectively respond to confusion or re-sistance when everyone takes time to remember and share the parish story; where it came from and where it is going. All share in carrying forward the mission of the Church. At this critical moment, it may help to remind others about why they are here, that they too are called to renew themselves in acts of loving, teaching, serving, and witnessing. In the end, it is the parishioners who are constant stewards of the parish mission.

2. Holding Up a Picture

Presenting the change visually can help people move forward. What are the pictures that have been painted portraying why the current pastor is leaving and who the new pastor is? People will want to know what the parish will look like after the transition. A clear picture of what is coming can reduce resistance. There are many metaphors about the in-between times for you to consider. It is important to listen to the language people use. Images carry a lot of energy, and they can be both positive and negative. For example, are people talking about "leaving a sinking ship" or about "discovering new territory"? Are people saying "our parish is really blooming" or "our parish is dying on the vine"?

Listen for the images people use when they talk about the new pastor's arrival. Are people using victim-talk? You may hear things such as "We are helpless. We are only parishioners. What can we do?" Other people may be taking ownership for their parish. "This is our parish. How do we welcome and work with this change?"

This would be a good time to think about your vision for your parish. What picture do you paint for yourself? For oth-ers? What are this parish's "Promised Land" visions? What would the best of all parishes look like: what would go on during weekends, evenings, summer, Lent? How would this parish challenge and support its young? Weekly you proclaim paschal mystery: Christ's living, dying, and rising. Now apply it to yourself. Create a safe space for people to ask, "What is dying here? What is rising? What is coming to be?"

All of these images carry energy and can shape people's emotions and experience. Listen to yourself. How are you engaging this conversation and what images can you suggest? What scenarios can you create with other key leaders? Never underestimate the power of a good story![5]

3. Developing a Plan

Make attractive transition plans for launching the new beginning. Realists and pragmatists will want assurance that a strategy is in place. They need to know that someone is thinking about the realities of the situation. Begin preparing the parish as soon as possible. This step, done in collaboration with the departing pastor and staff, is one worth extensive conversation and consideration.

Create short-term wins. The parish may need an emotional boost. Work to accomplish objectives that help the parish through this time, while ensuring that parish activities and programs continue. Create highly visible, short-term goals that energize the community. For instance, consider creating a transition team, perhaps a delegation of parishioners and parish staff. Make sure communion calls are still being made, that the food pantry is well stocked, or that catechetical classes or Vacation Bible School continue to run. Make sure that people who provide liturgical ministries still receive their assignments. Moreover, ask what each of these ministries could do to enhance the parish's sending forth of the pastor who is leaving and the welcoming of the new pastor.

Develop welcome celebrations for the new pastor and prepare a welcoming environment. Find ways to capitalize on excitement to keep it going. Think about what would be meaningful for the parish and decide how parish leaders can assist in this.

Bring forward the past. Plan how to best present the character, personality, and needs of the parish to the new pastor. Create a parish profile and a way to tell the parish story from the parishioner perspective. Explore the parish's history, culture, and current realities. Discuss the core values, principles, customs, and traditions that make this parish unique. Describe the state of the parish and its unique gifts and contributions to the diocese, the immediate neighborhood, and the community at large. Name some of the challenges, too. Express willingness to entertain challenges such as financial stability or growing diversity.

Each parish has a personality that shapes both the members of the community and the community in which it resides. Bring this story forward. Your parish is unique and its own members can best describe that distinct identity. Even outsiders from the wider community might be able to contribute.

Anticipate the new. This is also the time to begin plans for receiving your new pastor. Sometimes this task is given to the parish pastoral council or a designated committee. If that occurs, it may be possible to work with your current pastor to contact the new pastor and learn what his hopes are for how he enters the community. Think about what would make the new pastor feel at ease and welcome. Prepare a welcome event, have flowers or welcome notes at his desk, set up a welcome sign at the rectory entrance. Propose a Sunday Mass at the time of transition with both pastors present.

4. Providing Parts to Play

There are many gifts within your community. Let yourself be surprised. This is a good opportunity to call forth those people not often enlisted. It is very important to reflect on how the change is affecting different groups and individuals in the parish and to think about how to respond to their needs. Don't underestimate people's desire to be involved. If there is a real sense of ownership of the parish, especially from longtime members, they are going to want to be involved in moving the parish forward.

Create significant roles for parishioners. As you work with the pastor and staff, ascertain who in the parish can best serve the community and how they might serve. Involve as many parishioners as possible in planning and participating in events and transition processes. Below are only a few examples of significant roles for parishioners. Be creative and involve as many people as possible. Listen to one another and find ways to work together.

- Find people in your community who have experienced parish transitions before, or perhaps corporate or even personal change, and who would be able to advise parish leaders.

- Call forth the members of the parish who would be good at keeping positive communications open with the community.

- Work with those who are good at understanding the rhythms of parish life and involve them in planning welcoming rituals and celebrations. Every parish has its share of wonderful cooks and bakers, musicians, and party planners!

> At present we see indistinctly, as in a mirror, but then face to face. At present I know partially; then I shall know fully, as I am fully known. So faith, hope, love remain, these three; but the greatest of these is love. *(1 Cor 13:12-13)*

- Invite everyone's participation in the ministry of prayer. Especially, don't forget the sick and shut-ins, people in nursing homes, and the elderly. Formally invite them, specifically, to be people of prayer for the community at this time.

- Create a short, positively worded prayer that every parish group can use when they gather or begin meetings.

What You Can Do

To assist your own sense of balance while moving through the middle ground, the following are strategies to help this be a time that is at least more curious than confusing:

Keep an open mind. Don't be afraid of your—or others'—emotions. Encourage questions. If Thomas had not expressed his doubts, would Jesus have been able to address them? Probably, Thomas spoke what others were thinking.

Look at your strengths and gifts. Offer them in areas that can be most helpful.

Find strength in partnering with parishioners and parish groups. This is a time for cultivating and developing positive working relationships.

Have the courage to evaluate your role in the parish and whether or not you want to continue in the leadership position you currently hold.

Allow yourself to be comfortable with not knowing how it's all going to turn out for you. During these days and months, give thanks for "treadmill time." When it seems nothing is happening, stay in for the long haul. Be patient with the transition and those moving through it. Nurture an open mind and open heart, even if you are sad about the change. Remember how much you love this community, and resolve to let go of what is not essential so that you can focus and serve, witnessing to and drawing strength from the great virtues of faith, hope, and love.

Questions for Personal Reflection

1. Am I balancing time looking back and grieving the loss, so that I can then move forward?

2. Do I feel guilty about accepting the change? If so, do I understand why?

3. Am I moving forward too slowly?

4. Am I moving forward too fast, in order to avoid the discomfort of this middle ground?

5. Can I creatively envision possibilities for the future?

6. Can I name how I want to be involved at this stage?

Questions for Group Discussion

1. Where is the Spirit inviting the parish to go? Can we take time to be curious about what "is wanting" to happen in the parish?

2. How can parish leadership work with the pastor and staff to move forward in ways that are respectful to the new pastor?

3. Has a parish transition plan been developed so that parish life can continue as we await the new pastor's arrival? How shall we communicate the plan to the parish?

4. When and how should the transition committee provide updates?

5. Can we develop a parish profile or way of recognizing the history and culture of our parish?

6. Have we participated in any diocesan offerings provided to assist the parish in this transition?

7. Has the parish ensured programming, liturgies, and essential obligations are being met?

8. What is our vision for how this change ought to come about?

9. Have we reached out to pastor, staff members, all the groups we serve?

Notes

1. Bridges, 60.

2. Bridges, 60. Dr. Bridges lists these four agenda as the principle engines that help people launch into a new beginning. We raise them here because, as questions of meaning, purpose, and role, they can reorient people to parish mission and help them regain a sense of personal control and active participation.

3. Marti R. Jewell and David A. Ramey, *The Changing Face of Church: Emerging Models of Parish Leadership* (Chicago: Loyola Press, 2010), 71.

4. Jewell and Ramey, 16.

5. John P. Kotter and Dan S. Cohen, *The Heart of Change: Real Life Stories of How People Change Their Organizations* (Boston: Harvard Business School Press, 2002), 80.

Launching New Beginnings

Beginnings come slowly. We live into them. One day you realize that you have stopped saying "We have a new pastor" and are simply talking about "our parish." You will find that you have come to the realization that things are not going back to the way they were and the change—the new pastor—is here to stay.

You may find yourself walking the narrow line between dreaming of possibilities for your parish and being a realist about what is possible. While much will depend on the leadership style, relational talents, skills, and vision of the new pastor, the parish is a system, and your actions and responses will also affect the outcome of this transition. In the days and months ahead, the culture of your parish will evolve in some way. There will be a new spirit and a new direction. It is important to understand that you and the rest of the parish can positively influence the new life that is inviting you forward.

How do new beginnings typically proceed? There is no one way they happen. Beginnings are organic, and transition is a process, not a moment in time. In some ways your new beginning started when you first heard the announcement of the transition, and it will certainly continue for quite some time. Initially, a priority for parish leaders during this phase is ensuring the quality of the parish's welcome of the new pastor. Welcome events are gateways to a period of reception in the days and months to come as pastor, staff, and community live their way into the new beginnings.

So how do you know when you have moved into the new beginning if, aside from the new pastor's arrival, there is no start date? Think of the process of growing a plant from a seedling. Plants take time to establish themselves, sending down roots you can't see, and then flourishing. People are going to be asked to accept the fact that things are different now. An experienced gardener once said of new plantings that first they sleep, then they creep, and finally they leap. Parishioner leaders are critically important as a positive force, nurturing the new beginnings in your community. There are people who need tending, including the pastor and staff and, in many different ways, each and every parishioner!

Committing to the Journey

Life under the leadership of a new pastor takes time to develop. Most priests have heard the admonition to move slowly and learn the culture of the parish before making any changes. The new pastor will want to get to know the members of the parish, meet the staff and parish leaders, and learn what is needed. Allowing this change to develop in its own time will require a spiritual commitment from you as the parish moves forward. William Bridges suggests several "rules" for this phase, which we interpret below for the parish setting:[1]

> I continue my pursuit toward the goal, the prize of God's upward calling, in Christ Jesus.   *(Phil 3:14)*

Be consistent. As the new pastor settles in, much will be required of each member of the parish, especially those with leadership responsibilities. Remember what you discovered about the purpose of the parish, its mission, and its challenges. Keep your eyes on the prize, as St. Paul invites us.

Ensure that life goes on. Monitor, assess, and support programs and services within your purview. Look for and point out achievements, even of small tasks, and progress. Use strategies at the end of this guide (see page 39), assuring the community that services and routines continue during the transition.

Ritualize the new beginning. As Catholics we ritualize well. Take the opportunity to create liturgical and non-liturgical celebrations that welcome your arriving pastor and acknowledge the new journey you will undertake together.

Celebrate the milestone. Help people know that their efforts to bring the parish through the transition were noticed and are well appreciated! Through everything from small moments of personal conversation and thank-you notes to appreciation gatherings, you are helping people know that their presence is valued and counted on.

Recognizing That People Are Unique

Parishioners will continue to experience a variety of emotions at this time. You may experience their expressions of hope and enthusiasm as well as caution. Pastoral and practical questions that surfaced when the transition was announced will now beg for answers. Some people will be impatient, ready to move on so that everything is back to "normal." Remember, if you have been working with this transition for a while, you may need to recognize that some parishioners are in different places than you. They must move through all the stages in their own time and way.

Finally, there is little to be gained in comparing the new with the old. No matter how hard people try to keep everything as it was, there still will be differences, maybe not at first, but over time. The change may or may not be what you are looking for, but it may be very welcome to others who were not happy in the past.

Confusion and resistance are likely to keep showing up. Notice when they do and recognize them for what they are, ways for us to catch up with the change. Resistance happens in so many ways, and whether we realize it or not, our individual actions do impact the whole. Skeptics can be passive-aggressive. Those who have low tolerance for change may drag their feet.

Here are some ways people resist. You may think of others.

- Withdrawing and isolating—not being part of the new beginnings.

- Holding unrealistic expectations of what can happen.

- Sharing gossip and repeating rumors.

- Holding on to the past.

- Thinking about one's personal needs only, losing awareness of the community.

- Withholding information from leaders, staff, or pastor.

- Not being able to welcome, express openness or flexibility.

- Remembering and talking about the pastor you had, or the parish under his leadership, as if everything had been ideal.

Déjà Vu All Over Again

In some very real ways, and even in yourself, the perception at this "New Beginnings" stage may be that you're all back at "Endings." In the obvious absence of the former pastor, in the person of the new pastor, in even the smallest new practices and operations he initiates, reality comes calling. "We knew he'd be different, but . . ."

Remember that all three stages are always present to a community in some way. Your new pastor may have been reading the pastor's book in this series, or he may well know that it's a time of true endings as well as new beginnings for the community. Pastors say they too are dealing with loss and endings personally at this time: "Well, I'm not in St. Bertha's anymore. . . ." It will be good for everyone to give themselves and others some slack, and in some areas of life, actually permit, declare, and even encourage middle-ground practices.

It bears saying again, it is up to you how you will participate. This is the parish's chance to move forward, engaging creativity and new possibilities. You can model your commitment to the future of your parish by being pastoral and caring in the days and months ahead. Find those willing to hold the community in love and prayer and be a steadfast presence. Your new pastor has the right and even the duty to bring new insights and vision. As you blend in

> The fruit of the Spirit is love, joy, peace, patience, kindness, generosity, faithfulness, gentleness, self-control. Against such there is no law.
> *(Gal 5:22-23)*

your discernments about what the parish can be, momentum can build. Good dialogue among pastor, staff, and parishioners will lead to the unfolding of a vitally alive parish.

What You Can Do

Even if you personally experience some ambivalence, you will discover that despite all of the bargaining, the change has really happened. Now you must find a way to live into it. As in any new relationship, building rapport with a new pastor will take time. There will be a "getting to know you" phase in which you test your previous beliefs or assumptions about the new pastor and what he brings to the parish—and he of you! This is followed predictably by that period in which you and the pastor get to know each other. A healthy practice is to entertain "best case" scenarios, and to play them out in your reflection and prayer time. What can follow is a growing pastoral relationship. That can lead to mutual discovery of collaborative ways to serve the parish together.

It is possible that you already knew the man who would become your new pastor. You may have worked with him before. If so, resolve to allow him to be different in this new setting and ask the same courtesy of him. You may want to let this become a new chapter in the relationship during which you can both serve well.

As a parish leader you have undertaken the responsibility to move beyond addressing your own needs. Think about how you want to be a part of facilitating the new life and stability of the parish. Is this a time to continue in your leadership role? Does a different way of serving beckon? Self-care precedes good leadership. This might be a great time to seek outside counsel, preferably from someone who knows you well but is not herself or himself a stakeholder in the parish.

Questions for Personal Reflection

1. What is going on in my mind and heart?

2. How do I want to be part of this new time in the life of my parish?

3. Do I still belong in a leadership role in this parish?

4. If I decide to move on, what are my reasons for doing so?

5. If I stay, what is my motivation? Am I doing it for the good of the parish?

6. Whichever decision I make, can I do it with integrity and energy?

7. Was I ready to move on before the announcement of the transition? If so, can I still honor that?

8. Am I clear about my own expectations of the new pastor? Of myself? For the parish?

9. Who might be a trusted advisor, one who hasn't been involved with the transition?

10. What do I need from my new pastor in order to fulfill my leadership role? What will he need from me?

11. How can I work with my faith community as a whole?

Questions for Group Discussion

1. Are we providing steady reassurance as the transition moves forward?

2. Is adequate communication continuing? Where are any gaps or needs?

3. Are rituals and celebrations in place for welcoming the new pastor?

4. In consultation with the pastor and staff, have we developed symbols or rituals for bringing the past forward and opening to new possibilities?

5. Are there ways we are reexperiencing "endings" or a sense of returning to middle ground?

6. Are we envisioning possibilities for the future of the parish?

Notes

1. Bridges, 69. Dr. Bridges identifies the rules with four admonitions: Be consistent. Ensure quick successes. Symbolize the new identity. Celebrate the success.

Frequently Asked Questions

What are some things I need to know about a new pastor?

Both the departing pastor and the arriving one will be going through their own transition process. Even if your new pastor is excited about coming to your parish, he may be leaving a place that was very life-giving for him. Leaving an assignment where he was particularly happy adds, of course, to his sense of loss. He is leaving behind people he came to know well, with whom he knew how to work.

A new pastor doesn't really know how he will be received, and may not know what parish challenges he will face. While he may come in with a strong, calm presence, he still has many new people to meet and a whole parish history, culture, and social dynamics to learn. All of this takes time.

If a priest enters a parish where the previous pastor was dearly loved, he may find himself resented for not being "him." If his leadership style is noticeably different from his predecessor, the adjustment can become all the more difficult. On the other hand, if the previous pastor was not so well received, the new pastor may need additional time to gain parishioners' trust. This is where a good understanding of the parish will help you know how to support an arriving pastor.

If the new pastor is also a first-time pastor, the process can be complicated by transition to a new role as well as to a new parish. Even in the best of all worlds, a first-time pastor's anticipation about being a pastor will not match perfectly with the realities of your new parish. Can the parish help him establish this new identity in a respectful way and be patient as he "tests his wings"?

What are some things I can do to get started with the new pastor?

There are some basic things you can do if you want to develop a relationship with the new pastor. You will want to take the initiative. Remember, he is meeting many parishioners for the first time. Some suggestions you might think about:

- Begin by developing a relationship.

- Refrain from presenting him with a list of what he needs to do.

- Resist quick judgments.

- Give him a fair chance to ask questions or to observe and learn.

- Give him time.

- Be open and willing to learn and adapt.

Am I being disloyal to my old pastor if I get along with the new one?

The answer to this question is emphatically "No." While the relationship with the previous pastor may feel awkward at first, your care for him can be a marker for what is possible with the new pastor. Remember, you are not replacing your previous pastor in your affections. You are instead working to develop a new relationship, and it will have its own unique qualities.

Can I call my previous pastor for advice?

Generally this is not a good idea. Allow some distance for a while. While you may want to continue your friendship, your pastor is moving on with his life and can no longer make or influence decisions in your parish. You will want to avoid "triangling," a way of trying to get the previous pastor involved in problems with expectations that he can short-circuit the system. He cannot. That is not in his purview and should not be expected.

Can I invite my previous pastor back to the parish to preside at a baptism or wedding?

You will be asked to recognize that once the new pastor has arrived, it will be up to him to perform the sacramental and pastoral functions of the parish. Remember that the rhythms and rituals of parish life are not dependent on the person presiding but on the beauty and grace of the sacraments and liturgy themselves. It may be difficult at first to have someone new presiding, but in time it will become the new normal.

What are some things I might need to know about the parish staff?

Most staff will want to work with parishioners and care for the community through the transition. They will want to be there for the parish, providing what stability and continuity of programming and presence they can. It will be helpful for you to continue to work with them in order to move the parish forward through this time.

At the same time, the staff will be dealing with their own series of concerns during the transition. They may feel a little disoriented and emotionally guarded, as his transition affects their livelihood as well as their faith life. Some may wonder if the new pastor will want them to continue serving in the parish. As their supervisor the new pastor may keep the staff functioning as they are or perhaps rearrange their responsibilities or the manner in which they have access to the pastor. All of this will take some time. So, while the staff may be the stable factor in the transition for parishioners, they may not be feeling all that stable themselves. They must do their own work in this change.

It is wise not to make assumptions about what staff persons know or can do. They may not have any more information about what is happening than you. Offer support. Offer to work with them to develop whatever short-term goals need to be in place so that the work and ministry of the parish can continue through this time.

What is the role of the parish pastoral council?

The parish council is in place to be a consultative body to the pastor. Clarity and consistency in this role will be very helpful to the parish. It would be helpful to review the council's mission or charter documents. Be available for both the pastor and parishioners to bring concerns and questions, as the council at this time can be an effective clearinghouse for issues and priorities. Upon his arrival, seek to establish a relationship of mutual respect with the new pastor, so that the chairperson, the executive committee, and members are able to be clear about their roles.

Can I contact the diocese?

The bishop, diocesan agencies, and priest personnel always welcome your inquiries. However, be sure that what you are concerned about deserves to be addressed at this level. Calling about personal dislikes and disappointments is not appropriate. First, determine whether there are truly serious issues. Then attempt to resolve the matter with the appropriate parish leaders. Consider sharing your concerns with the new pastor, the parish pastoral council, or with the parish staff. Parishes operate under the principle of "subsidiarity" which suggests that all issues be resolved at the most immediate or lowest level whenever possible. If resolution fails, you may then need to contact the appropriate diocesan office for guidance.

How can I take care of myself during this transition?

As a parish leader you will be asked a lot of questions, hear a lot of rumors, perhaps need to wipe away a few tears of joy, sorrow, or anger. However, even as you cope with your own feelings, your role includes participation in developing and sharing a vision for how the entire parish can move forward. To contribute effectively, you need to take care of yourself. Here are three suggestions:

1. *Find ways to be present to the community even as you set good boundaries.* Decide what you are willing to participate in, listen to, and be available for. Expectations placed on you

as a parish leader must be limited and reasonable, but only you can hold your boundaries.

2. *Be patient with yourself and allow yourself to move through all the phases and emotions that will come to you.* These are normal experiences. Try not to project them onto other people. It is important to engage in self-reflection and remain aware of how you yourself are feeling.

3. *Be the change you wish to see.* Too often people give away their power and think that everything depends on someone else. In a system as important as a parish, everyone matters. Are you showing enthusiasm? Concern? Energy? Commitment? Trust? Honesty? Integrity?

Remember too, this does not all rest on your shoulders. This new beginning belongs to the entire parish. Have appropriate conversations with families and friends. If that is not enough, you may want to find other resources, whether books or persons who can help in the sorting out and managing.

What are my options if I cannot see myself getting along with the new pastor?

When all is said and done, not everyone may be happy with how the transition is proceeding. If you are one who cannot see yourself continuing with things as they are and find yourself unhappy, give yourself permission to explore a variety of options.

As you move forward it will be important to respect the authority of the new pastor and of the office he holds. How you honor yourself, the pastor, and your community will make a difference in how you proceed with your discernment.

Take time. Start by giving the transition time. Once things have settled down, take a second look. Remember you may be grieving. Work through your sense of loss. Be gentle with yourself. Grieving follows an unpredictable timeline. Allow it to work itself out, and share with someone who can assure you the safe space you need to test realities and name feelings, as there could be a variety of confusing emotions. Take time for prayer and reflection. Consider what God might be wanting for you and for your community. This may not be obvious at first. Take time in prayer to sort it all out.

Remember that you are part of a community. While you may have played a significant role or have definite ideas about what needs to happen, you are part of a larger community with needs that will not always align with your own. Decide whether, when, and how you can balance the needs of the larger community with your own.

Don't participate in parking lot gossip! Whether you like what is happening or not, avoid conversations that only raise emotion but solve little. When you speak with other parish leaders or parishioners, be as clear as you are able to be about your concerns and then seek to work together in order to find solutions. Try to avoid comparisons with the departing pastor or share unflattering stories about his pastoring. Avoid entertaining assumptions about the new pastor or his motives.

Anticipate the experience and skill level of the new pastor. There are many questions to be considered as the new pastor moves in. Is he a longtime pastor or brand new in the role? Has he worked in a parish the size of yours before? What might be different about your parish from his previous assignment? Can you allow him a learning curve, and how can you assist in that learning? Different people bring different leadership styles. Would a conversation with the new pastor about the style be helpful to you? It is always better not to assume you know or understand the reasons for his actions. What might be mistaken for arrogance, for instance, might really be shyness or nervousness.

Recognize the new relationship. No matter how well you got along with your previous pastor, do not assume that your relationship with the new pastor will be the same. Relationships must be built over time and will be unique to the people involved. Show your willingness to be available, offer your time and talent. Don't try to recreate what you had with the previous pastor. Let this new relationship develop in its own way.

Initiate dialogue. Start by having some conversation with the chair of parish pastoral council. If you determine you need to meet with the pastor, make an appointment. Begin your meeting with the pastor by clearly stating why you asked for the appointment. Be clear that you are representing only yourself. Name the reasons as objectively as possible. Keep the tone respectful, leaving room for him to form his own questions or response. If you sense defensiveness, be clear about your intention. Emphasize that you want to work to understand as well as be understood.

Consider different ways of participating. Consider working in the new system, but in a different capacity, stepping away from your current leadership role. Acknowledge the possibility that, for any number of reasons, you may not be able to continue as you have in the past. There are many ways to be involved in a parish. Whether some of them are highly visible or less noticeable, all matter.

What do we do if we experience frequent pastor changes?

Work to build trust within the community. This is a time for the presence and modeling of parish leaders, perhaps also a time to promote healing. A leader's work is to assure the community that life goes on but also to explore how to work with a new, even if temporary, pastor or administrator.

Remember the purpose of the parish: to call forth disciples who will care for one another, drawing from the love of Jesus and carrying out the mission of Church. This must continue.

Build a culture of mutuality and reliance. Seek to depend on one another.

> "Do to others whatever you would have them do to you."
> *(Matt 7:12)*

Consider bringing in professionals who can help build strategies for healing and reconnecting with the Church and parish mission.

Strategies for Effective Transition

In this final section of the guide you will find a variety of suggestions for moving through your pastor transition. Most ideas come from parish leaders and pastors of parishes who underwent a recent pastor transition. Be selective! You do not need to use all of these ideas, and be mindful that this list is incomplete. These ideas and lists provide conversation starters for you as you make your own transition plans.

There He Goes! Saying Good-bye to Your Current Pastor

Milestone One: Observing and Maintaining the Calendar

- Ensure parish routines.

- Put programs and calendars in place so that parish life can continue as normally as possible through the transition.

- Decide what must be done now, what needs to be changed, and what may not be necessary during this time.

- Continue rituals and activities that are important to the stability and self-identity of the parish.

Milestone Two: Saying Good-bye

- Develop farewell rituals and celebrations for the departing pastor.

- Plan a farewell liturgy.
- Host a Sunday breakfast or picnic after the Masses.
- Plan an evening party with a potluck dinner and music.
- Engage the parish council in planning these events and rituals, asking them to work in collaboration with the staff and departing pastor.
- Work with smaller groups, such as the school or the formation program, to plan personalized farewell events.

- Offer meaningful gifts and mementos of the parish to the departing pastor.

  - Create a memory book or memory "suitcase."
  - Decide on a meaningful gift, plaque, or other token of appreciation.

Milestone Three: Transition Planning

- Do strategic planning for the transition.

  - Create parishioner transition teams using members from existing groups: councils, commissions, boards, and so on. Consider including people from other groups, such as catechists, choir members, members of the youth group, or other parish organizations.
  - Develop a transition plan for the parish.
  - Bring in speakers and consultants to provide transition training sessions.
  - Facilitate parish meetings and conversations.

- Provide directives to the transition committee.

  - Develop a parish transition plan in consultation with the pastor.
  - Ensure continuous communication with the parish as the transition proceeds.
  - Involve as many people as possible in the transition.

- Create a parish profile on the history and state of the parish for the new pastor. Include:
  - Parish mission statement, demographics, financials;
  - Major events in the parish memory or self-image;
  - Significant information, data, calendars, rituals, and traditions;
  - Information about significant upcoming financial, structural, or other issues.
- Plan for completion of any parish projects, such as fund drives, renovations, special programs, and so on.

Here We Go! Awaiting a New Pastor

Milestone Four: Caring for the Parish Community

- Focus on timely communication.
  - Begin intentional, regular, and frequent communication with parishioners.
  - Hold parish information evenings to let people know what the process and timeline will be for determining a new pastor.
  - Host town hall meetings to provide parishioners a place to share their thoughts, ideas, concerns, and feelings, but be realistic about the purpose of the gathering.
  - Conduct parish surveys to identify parishioners' concerns and particular aspects of the parish culture that people believe are important to maintain.

Milestone Five: Working with the Diocese

- Anticipate parish needs in a new pastor.
  - Develop a parish profile that includes information about the culture of the parish, its "heart," and the skills of its parishioners.

- Consult the parish staff to ascertain and document specific needs in a new pastor: bilingual ability? financially astute? able to work with social issues?

- Collaborate with your pastor to engage diocesan representatives who may be available to the parish.
  - Participate in any diocesan information/training/transition events available to you.
  - Form recommendations if there is a diocesan agency that receives parishioner input.
  - Offer a parish consultation night and invite representatives from the diocese.

He's Here! Getting to Know the New Pastor

Milestone Six: Welcoming the New Pastor

- Prepare for the new pastor's arrival.
  - Ensure that the parish offices and rectory are clean, maybe even freshly painted, appropriately furnished, and inviting. For significant renovations or redecorating, consult with the new pastor first.
  - Place flowers or a cake or other snacks in the rectory office on the day of his arrival. Little things go a long way.
  - Create "A Taste of the Parish"—a binder or other visual presentation that can be waiting for him when he arrives.
  - Extend an invitation to meet with the parish council and finance council.
  - Create a welcome sign.
  - Put a welcome announcement in the parish bulletin.

- Anticipate possible needs or concerns of the new pastor.
  - Make necessary information available, such as Mass schedules, server and choir schedules, information about parish meetings, and so on.

- Extend personal invitations to your meetings/events/homes, but allow him to set his own pace for getting to know people.
- Seek ways and resources to assist the pastor in bridging the gap if there are cultural or ethnic differences between him and the parish community.
- Create parishioner nametags.
- Ask parishioners to wear nametags at receptions and Masses.
- Provide an orientation to parish councils, commissions, boards, and committees.
- Help him acclimate to the neighborhood and neighboring churches.
- Offer information or even a short tour to help him feel "at home."

- Create welcoming events.
  - Host a "Meet the Pastor" event.
  - Ask parish lay leaders to be present at town hall meetings and other parish gatherings.
  - Host a welcome event after his first Mass, such as coffee and donuts or parish picnic.
  - Print an introduction letter from the new pastor in a parish newsletter or bulletin.
  - Plan receptions, blessings, and compose parishioner prayer.
  - Plan the installation liturgy in conjunction with the bishop, vicar general, or vicariate dean.

Milestone Seven: Moving Forward

- Evaluate the parish mission.
  - Create opportunities for parishioners to share with each other and with the new pastor their dreams and hopes.
  - Join the pastor, staff, and community in identifying assets and opportunities.

- Discover where new energy might be and whether there could be new directions for the parish.
- Prepare for major liturgical seasons.
  - Notify parishioners if there will be any changes in major celebrations.
  - Acknowledge that people may struggle with some changes.

Quick Checklists

Seven Milestones for Pastor Transition

- Observe and maintain the calendar.
- Care for the parish community.
- Say good-bye to the departing pastor.
- Work with the diocese.
- Transition with the community.
- Welcome the new pastor.
- Move forward.

Three Things to Know about Change Dynamics in Communities

- There is an anticipated pattern of endings, middle ground, and new beginnings.
- Each phase of the transition has its own tasks. You will need to say good-bye well, ensure that parish life continues, and move forward.
- Everyone in the parish will experience the transition, but individuals will respond in their own way. Communication, care, and connection need high priority.

Strategies for Parish Leaders During Transition

- Be involved.

- Communicate with the parish as the transition proceeds.

- Develop short-term goals to keep the parish going during the transition.

- Be present to the parish with an open mind and an open heart.

- Anticipate change. Be flexible and patient.

- Work with the parish staff and diocesan representatives.

- Evaluate your own involvement and how you want to be present to the parish as it goes forward.

Five Ways to Help the Departing Pastor Prepare His Leave-taking

- Plan farewell events, final liturgies, and gifts.

- Don't disconnect too quickly! He is not gone until he is gone.

- Complete work begun under this pastor where possible.

- When it is time, let him go! Don't make this transition harder than it has to be.

- Get on with life. Show him that you are able to continue on your own.

Five Parishioner Ministries to the New Pastor

- Prepare information the new pastor will need to get started. Include things such as major chairpersons; committees and their functions; major upcoming events; meeting schedules; job descriptions for staff and significant volunteer roles; liturgical schedules; confession times; and so on.

- Prepare a welcoming environment in offices and rectory.

- Plan a warm welcome.

- Be available to meet with him.

- Be open to new possibilities, and don't cling to the past.

Bibliography

Bridges, William. *Managing Transitions: Making the Most of Change*, 3rd ed. Cambridge: Da Capo Press, 2009.

———."Change, Transitions, and How to Navigate Them," http://www.strategies-for-managing-change.com/william-bridges.html.

Ganim, Carole, ed. *Shaping Catholic Parishes: Pastoral Leaders in the 21st Century*. Chicago: Loyola Press, 2008.

Jewell, Marti R. and David A. Ramey. *The Changing Face of Church: Emerging Models of Parish Leadership*. Chicago: Loyola Press, 2010.

Kotter, John P. and Dan S. Cohen. *The Heart of Change: Real Life Stories of How People Change Their Organizations*. Boston: Harvard Business School Press, 2002.